THE
DIVINE
KNOWING

THE
DIVINE
KNOWING:

Accepting the open invitation to grow in the knowledge of God

Bailey J. Doty

CONTENTS

PREFACE

God has apprehended my heart. I was born again at four years old, but only in the last few years have I realized just how available Jesus is—how near He is, how deeply He desires relationship with us, and how He still speaks to us today. Because of that revelation, I have never been the same. My motivations in writing this book were to make others aware of the Lord's invitation to know Him and to be a faithful steward of the message to the Body I believe Holy Spirit has entrusted me with. Growing in the knowledge of God is a lifelong journey that I have only just begun, but so far it has been the most thrilling, fulfilling undertaking.

I wrote this book to the Body of Christ. I wrote this book for those who, like me, grew up in the church; those who might be born again and grew up hearing about Jesus and reading their Bibles, but have never realized or need a reminder of the relational intimacy available with Jesus in this earthly life. I believe we are on the brink of one of the greatest moves of God the world has ever seen. And the Father wants us as His Church to be prepared for such a move—He wants us to be able to recognize Him when He comes. It is a recognition that will only come through time spent in intimacy with Him.

Please read this book alongside your Bible. I reference many verses, but often not directly. My hope in incorporating Scripture in this way is for readers to get into the Word for themselves and to have revelations of God's nature on a personal level. He wants YOU to really, truly know Him for yourself.

Thank you for reading my book. I believe it is a divine set-up that you are doing so. The Lord loves you more than you can imagine—His longing is for you to live a life of experiential knowledge of Him. I bless you in your journey of discovering Who He is, and I ask the Father that He gives you "the Spirit of wisdom and revelation that you might know Him better." (Ephesians 1:17, NIV)

Bailey J. Doty

CHAPTER ONE:
INVITATION

A longing inexpressible exists within every human soul. At times more pronounced than others but never ceasing to linger and plague our present, that aching "almost"—a nostalgia with origins hard to remember—is the eternity hidden in our hearts.[1] The Creator placed it inside us with a purpose. He intends to draw all people to Himself,[2] and that void prompts us to pursue Him, for it cannot be filled with anything other than His Spirit. This engrained, heavenly homesickness is the internal lure that keeps us locked into the righteous straight and narrow[3] if we surrender to it.

While born-again believers may have identified the Source of such a longing, and although they have found freedom from their pasts and hope for their eternity through blood-bought salvation,[4] they never comepletely lose the longing. Some chalk it up as inevitable unfulfillment until the afterlife, which may be partially true. But the fullness realized only after we die should not hinder us from taking hold of the full life[5] Jesus promised us in this earthly "now." Our deepest, truest longing is not for a final resting place, but a Person. We desire Jesus. Communion with Him is our most fundamental fulfillment. And there is *more*, so much

---

[1] Ecclesiastes 3:11
[2] John 12:32
[3] Matthew 7:13-14
[4] Matthew 26:28; Hebrews 9:14
[5] John 10:10

more of God to be discovered. In fact, in our time and in this season, the Lord is introducing Himself to His Bride afresh by extending an invitation to grow in the knowledge of God.

To position His people for that reintroduction, the Holy Spirit is stirring up hunger, a divine discontentment within the Church. A hunger for authentic, raw relationship with Jesus; a discontentment with controlled, lifeless religion. He has been placing His finger upon the First-Love longing within us, magnifying it so that we might be prompted to reach out like children and find Him.[6] God can be found. He is a substantive, tangible Father. As such, He wishes to engage with us through all the same faculties we use to engage anything else in life: our minds, our hearts, our spirits, our five senses. Intimate engagement with Him on every level of our being grows our knowledge of God.

Knowledge of God is not limited to our minds' capacity to comprehend Him. Of course, God cares about our intellects and the soundness of our theology; however, knowing *about* God is completely different than actually *knowing* Him. If they were the same, the Pharisees would have been the closest to Jesus, but they missed Him in the flesh among them—they overlooked scriptures' invitation for intimate, experiential knowledge of the Messiah.[7] Filling our minds with "facts" about God without opening our hearts to Him is backsliding into the very alienation Christ died to eradicate.[8]

Disregarding hunger's nudge in our spirits means settling for admiration of God from a distance and

---

[6] Acts 17:27
[7] John 5:39-40
[8] Colossians 1:21-23

disconnection from the Vine, our sole Lifeline. Many believers, although they have secured eternal redemption, live powerless, fruitless lives[9] because of apathy and their attempts to fulfill the longing with anything other than the Lord. There is more than one type of death—even believers can live in deterioration, for the Lord warns that His people perish when they do not know Him.[10]

To live without knowing Him is to miss our destiny. If we stay unacquainted with the Shepherd's voice,[11] we render ourselves susceptible to the voice of a stranger[12]— our souls' enemy, who ever tries to isolate us from God by causing us to question His nature or by convincing us that we are capable of finding fulfillment in something other than the Spirit. Going down that path ends in malnourishment and the longing never lifts; it remains and deepens, often misdiagnosed as things like depression, anxiety, unhappiness, and hopelessness. God will not be contained within the "manageable," bite-sized portions of our lives we attempt to reduce Him to, like the two-hour parameter of a Sunday service. He is an all-or-nothing God. Our knowledge of Him will not grow in the confines of double-mindedness. Christians who ignore the Lord's invitation to know Him in a real way will only have just enough of God to be discontent.

Holy Spirit igniting hunger within us is not meant to be a torment, but a *kindness*. Hunger makes us desperate enough to hope that God will satisfy our hearts' yearnings, compelling us to go to Him for refreshing.[13]

---

[9] John 15:5
[10] Hosea 4:6
[11] John 10:1-15
[12] John 10:5
[13] John 7:37

While placing our hopes of fulfillment in the wrong sources leads to heartsickness, having our longings for the Lord fulfilled by Him is a sweet-to-the-soul tree of life.[14] God allowed Adam and Eve to eat of the tree of life within the context of knowing Him intimately. In the same way, God will give us the right to partake of that tree again[15]—the tree whose fruit enlightens the eyes of our heart to see Him more clearly and live a purpose-filled life—when we embrace righteousness [16] and abandon ourselves unto knowing Him intimately. Eating of the tree of life is the antidote for a perishing soul, and He intends to reinstate everything lost in the Fall. And that is why genuine knowledge of God cannot be solely intellectual. Rather, it is a love affair with the Lord: an experiential knowledge developed by accepting His invitation to taste and see Who He is,[17] living off the fruit of the tree of life that flourishes within our secret-place gardens. Truly, He joyfully satisfies every longing within us, so our hunger should be seen as a sign of spiritual health and upcoming blessing—Jesus promises the hungry will be fed[18] and satisfied with good things.[19]

***

We must remember that knowing God is an open invitation, not an endeavor reserved for the chosen few. Not only can He be known by everyone, He *wants* to be known. The Lord is not a stingy tease. He promises He

---

[14] Proverbs 13:12, 19
[15] Revelation 2:7
[16] Proverbs 11:30
[17] Psalm 34:8
[18] Matthew 5:6
[19] Psalm 103:5

would not have told us to seek Him if He could not be found.[20] God's love is loud and unashamed in its pursuit of us. The hunger rising inside us testifies to God giving us hearts to know Him, as He longs for us to return to Him.[21] The Father desires to expand our knowledge of Him beyond merely knowing the deeds He does for us, while yet important, and make known His ways to us, like He did in the life of His friend, Moses.[22] The Lord's ways are the deeper why's of His deeds—they are His heart's dreams and subtleties only discovered through intimate time spent, always pointing to Who He is in unchanging nature.

Our God, the Supreme Being in the universe, invites us into friendship and beckons us into the infinite, eternal treasure hunt that is learning His ways. While beyond comprehension, we cannot afford to pass up the call, because we *can* miss it by ignoring our hunger and rejecting the invitation. Accepting His offer requires something of us.

Growing in the knowledge of God does not just "happen." It is an individual undertaking that necessitates intimate intentionality. No one else can love or know God for us, and even corporate gatherings are simply meant to be shared furtherances of the intimacy we as individuals enjoy with Holy Spirit in our day-to-day.

Perhaps we have lived in ignorance of what is available, never properly identifying the hunger of our hearts and settling for religion rather than relationship, but it is never too late to begin the journey. We begin

---

[20] Isaiah 45:19

[21] Jeremiah 24:7

[22] Psalm 103:7

learning His ways and thus walking in His paths[23] by using the gift of our free wills to choose Him. Love requires choice—God took a risk by giving us free will. It takes our wills to pray for ourselves what the Apostle Paul prayed for the Ephesian church: that the Lord would give us the Spirit of wisdom and revelation so we may know Him better.[24] That prayer should be the outflow of our hunger, the kindling of our childlike curiosity that causes us to wonder what He is like.

Intimacy is not established in a moment, and knowing God will not come through a lone encounter or one prayer. He must become our daily choice, our chief sustenance every second of each day. Knowing Him is a lifelong, but joyful commitment, especially when we realize His loving hold on us is stronger than we can imagine.

By choosing to accept His invitation and to steward our hunger to know Him, we find life, because we find Him. Christ is our life.[25] Who we are and what we were created for is discovered exclusively in the revelation of Who He is. Anything we learn about the nature of God becomes a binding anchor point of hope[26] and trust—we are vulnerable to the waves of circumstances and the winds of deception without it.[27]

Most importantly, revelations of God's nature bring us back into covenant with Him, which is God's intention in re-revealing Himself to His people. We are the "Beloved" in history's greatest love story, and the enemy forever tries to keep us from intimacy with our

---

[23] Isaiah 2:3
[24] Ephesians 1:17
[25] Colossians 3:4
[26] Hebrews 6:19
[27] Ephesians 4:13-14

Bridegroom. Growing in the knowledge of God is the enemy's greatest threat and our highest calling.

CHAPTER TWO:
NEARNESS

God gives us access to Himself. Not only *can* He be known, He *wants* to be known. Everything in the universe testifies to this fact. Everything within us was designed by Him and for Him,[1] created to be aware of Him, to know Him. The longing within us for the Lord is not a tease of what cannot be, but an indication of what is possible. It is our spirit's response to the ardent song eternally released over us by our Ultimate Love, Who eagerly knocks at the doors of our hearts. [2] Our understanding, slanted by years of worldly wisdom and past disappointments, might tell us otherwise, but the truth is: the Lord is near. [3] A revelation of His tremendous nearness is where life begins, the starting point for growing in the knowledge of God.

While God has forever been near in the sense of His omnipresence (His being everywhere at the same time;[4] His containment of the universe within Himself[5]), Jesus' death and resurrection ushered in a new covenant that restores us to God's original intention: the intimate nearness like Adam and Eve enjoyed with God in the Garden of Eden.[6] The blood of Jesus redeemed us from

---

[1] Colossians 1:16
[2] Revelation 3:20
[3] Philippians 4:5
[4] Proverbs 15:3; Psalm 139:7-10
[5] Colossians 1:17; 1 Kings 8:27
[6] Genesis 2 & 3

damnation and purified us from sin.[7] Relieving our burden of sin is amazing enough, but it was not God's paramount end in saving us. Redemption is "step one" of His deepest desire: He wants intimacy with us, from the here and now into forever. That is why the blood of Jesus not only cleanses us from sin, but also draws us near to God relationally,[8] giving us unfettered access into the Most Holy Place.[9]

Before Jesus' atoning sacrifice, God limited His manifest Presence amongst the people of Israel to a section of the Old Testament tabernacle called the Holy of Holies,[10] where only the priests were allowed to enter once a year to give a sacrifice that postponed punishment for sin. The entire ritual reminded humanity of its need for a savior, inability to save itself from the sin that was killing it, and chasmic separation from God. But within the ritual was a seed of hope—the promise of redemption and Eden-esque, relational unity with the Lord restored. Jesus, the Last Adam,[11] our Perfect High Priest,[12] and the only Way,[13] faced death on our behalf, receiving our punishment of God's wrath when He took our sin upon Himself. Because of that sacrificial act of Love, the veil that separated us from God has been rent in two.[14] We can now stand before Him, holy and blameless in His sight,[15] because the blood of Jesus covers us.

---

[7] 1 John 1:7
[8] Ephesians 2:13
[9] Hebrews 10:19
[10] Exodus 26
[11] 1 Corinthians 15:45
[12] Hebrews 4:14
[13] John 14:6
[14] Matthew 27:51
[15] Ephesians 1:4

This is the beautiful Gospel we, as those born-again, [16] should know and profess to believe. Unfortunately we too often do not live out the full implications of our salvation. Salvation was never meant to be a one-time prayer that gives us a free pass into heaven. It can start there, but He intends a lifelong, moment-to-moment covenant. Jesus is our Husband,[17] but we do not always treat Him as such. We can know all the right things to say—we "prayed the prayer" and use Christian lingo—and our hearts can still be far from Him.[18] He longs for our hearts to be as near to His as His heart is to ours. His relentless nearness despite our complacency is staggering; an authentic revelation of it would bring each of us to our knees. What is hindering the Church from more fully stepping into its role as the Bride of Christ? How do we grow in awareness and reciprocation of His nearness, accessing the greater knowledge of God available within it? Many things, but these two for sure: we need a renewed perception of eternal life and we must let go of compartmentalization.

Eternal life is not limited to after our earthly deaths, and heaven is not simply a paradise destination for those redeemed by Jesus. Heaven is not so much a place as it is a Person. It is Who He is. His Presence is heaven, which is why the Lamb Himself will be the heavenly city's temple and His glory will be its illumination.[19] Jesus did not teach that eternal life began after death, but that it was *knowing* the Father.[20] True eternal life is knowing God by experience. That life, that knowledge of Him, is

---

[16] John 3:3
[17] Ephesians 5:25-27
[18] Isaiah 29:13
[19] Revelation 21:22-23
[20] John 17:3

available the second we are born again, because Holy Spirit gives us access to the Father.[21] (We are filled with His Spirit upon rebirth,[22] Holy Spirit within us testifies about Jesus,[23] and every revelation of Jesus speaks of the Father's nature.[24] How mind-blowing that such a God makes His home inside of us!) Holy Spirit leads us through the torn veil and reminds our hearts of the love covenant we are in with God. The freedom-giving Spirit of God that dwells within us transforms us into Christ's image[25] and guides us into the full life Jesus promised.[26] His work within us begins in the context of our present, earthly lives. That is why Jesus instructed us to pray, "on earth as it is in heaven."[27] Our mandate is to partner with Him to pull the reality of heaven to earth, bringing an awareness of His Presence into the now of our time.

Heaven, in the sense of life after death, will simply be an ever-deepening continuation of what we are called to do here—growing in the knowledge of God in the context of worship-filled intimacy. To miss this fact is to miss His nearness, to miss His open arms waiting for us, and to miss His genuine interest in our daily lives. If we believe that relationship with God is confined to heaven (in the frameworks of another realm and our existence after we die, which of course He is present in both), we will postpone any expectancy or responsibility for relationship with Him in this life. Thus, complacency creeps in, and our lives become dull and unfulfilling—we have no other option but to simply "hold on" until we

---

[21] Ephesians 2:18
[22] 1 Corinthians 6:19
[23] John 15:26
[24] Matthew 11:27; John 17:26
[25] 2 Corinthians 3:17-18
[26] John 10:10
[27] Matthew 6:10

die. That view is more deism than the Christianity Jesus presented. And His nearness, with every aspect of His nature wonderfully wrapped within it, boldly contradicts this view of life. The nearness of God is not only realized in the "someday" of eternity, but is in fact intrinsic to our being new creations.

Not only do we have the Spirit of God dwelling within us, we are "in Christ."[28] We are encompassed by Who He is, completely surrounded and saturated in His Presence in every way. When we died to our old selves, our lives became hidden with Christ in God.[29] We are living in the divine unity Jesus prayed for.[30] But if we get caught up in the details of life, if the eyes of our hearts linger anywhere other than the heavenly realms where we are seated with Christ,[31] we lose perspective of His irrefutable nearness. Compartmentalization is the result of that loss in perspective.

A compartmentalized life is one that is chopped into sections with "appropriate" timeframes for certain activities. Such a worldview limits our interactions with and understanding of God to the church as a building or institution. We then believe God can only be accessed, felt, and/or spoken to in the context of a church service. Boxing in the Lord in that way welcomes in both immorality and shame. Immorality because we do things we probably would not do if we thought He was present, not knowing that He did not stay in our Sunday-morning box and He *is* there. Shame because we find it hard to believe our seemingly non-"spiritual" activities or occupations—like our hobbies, the mundane activities

---

[28] Romans 6:11, 8:1; Colossians 2:6-7

[29] Colossians 3:2

[30] John 17:20-23

[31] Colossians 3:2; Ephesians 2:6

necessary to life, and professions outside the church, like business or government, for example—are pleasing to God. But the truth is, He enjoys it all. He is present in every moment, every activity. Because Holy Spirit dwells within us, we have become the Most Holy Place, erasing the possibility of a secular-sacred divide. Everything we do in life is an act of worship, whether we realize it or not. We are worshippers by nature, and we decide Who or what our worship is directed towards.

The revelation that we are "in Christ" should bring us into the understanding that every part of our life is in Christ, as well. He is our life,[32] holding every part of our existence together and giving it purpose. Remaining conscious of the Lord's nearness in everything and renewing our minds with simple prayers like, "Thank You that You are here," throughout our days prevent compartmentalization and fragmentation. It keeps our heart in a constant posture of holy worship. From that place of health, we do everything through Him, with Him, and unto Him—His nearness becomes the dominant aspect of our existence.

***

His nearness does not demand perfection from us. Shame and religion pressure us to stay away, to ignore His Presence, until we "make ourselves presentable." That is a standard we will not live up to. We cannot fix ourselves, as much as the enemy might tell us otherwise. But the Lord, full of compassion and lovingkindness, cares. We can cast our anxieties and struggles on Him,[33]

---

[32] Colossians 3:4
[33] 1 Peter 5:7

and He will lovingly empower us to overcome anything. He will give us His rest.

While the rest He offers does not require self-help, it does require vulnerable honesty about our needs and the use of our free will to choose Him. We must trust, surrender, and respond to His invitation to "Come."[34] Grace and life[35] are available in the willful setting our faces towards Him.

Simple acknowledgement of Him is all it takes, and the Father quickly closes the gap. God always does, ever in pursuit of our hearts. He is the Father who runs to embrace us while we are still a long way off, cutting short our walks of shame with extravagant welcomes and reminders of who we really are.[36] He is the Good Shepherd, leaving the flock to search out the wayward ones, joyfully carrying them next to His heart when they are found.[37] The cross showed the lengths Jesus will go to save our souls, to keep us near to Him—our Friend's great love for us on display by His dying.[38] To this day Jesus remains closer than a brother.[39] His lovesick eyes are fixed upon us every moment of every day.

The same Spirit within us Who draws our heart to the Father also pulls the Father's heart towards us. It is a beautiful cycle that will take us deeper and deeper into the consuming vortex of God's love if we lean into it. But if we are passive, if we choose to ignore Him, we break covenant with the One Who jealously longs for the Spirit He has caused to dwell within us. There is no gray area:

---

[34] Matthew 11:28

[35] John 5:39-40

[36] Luke 15:20

[37] Matthew 18:12-14; Isaiah 40:11

[38] John 15:13

[39] Proverbs 18:24

we are either a friend of God or a friend of the world.[40] Yet because of His grace and mercy, we can turn back to Him no matter how we have related to Him in the past. *He is here*, in this very moment, waiting to see if we will notice His nearness, anticipating our response. Our faithful God's passionate affection and attention are directed at us. Jesus is more near and more real than any other thing we can discern with our senses. We belong to Him, and His desire is for us:[41] what will our response be?

---

[40] James 4:4-5
[41] Song of Songs 7:10

CHAPTER THREE:
STILLNESS

A revelation of God's nearness inspires many responses within the believing heart, and we should give ourselves over to every one of them—worship, service, wonder, passion; just to name a few. But there is a response Holy Spirit does not want this generation to miss: *stillness.* Stillness makes room for the Lord, allowing Him His proper place in our hearts. He is *God*—nothing can share the throne of our hearts with Him, especially not anxiety, busyness, unbelief, fear, or whatever else sets itself up against the knowledge of Him.[1] He reveals Himself, and a line is immediately drawn in the sand. We have a choice to make. Will we take the path of pride, rough with distrust and false senses of control? Or will we take the path of stillness, full of humble surrender and childlike trust? We were designed to know Him; therefore stillness is intrinsic to our make up. We simply need to be recalibrated to the covenant we were created for, and He is mercifully patient in that process.

There is more to stillness than we realize. While it can include aspects of our external reality, such as a lack of sound or a lack of movement, stillness is not necessarily limited to those things. God intends to take us deeper, beneath the surface into a state called "stillness of soul"—a state not characterized by an absence of something but an infilling by Someone.

---

[1] 2 Corinthians 10:5

Stillness of soul is a moment-to-moment practice, a lifestyle set on increasing awareness to His Presence.

While indeed a spiritual "practice," it is not the usual kind. It is not comprised of principles that lead us to Him—that would take us back into religious striving. Instead, stillness is our intentional, daily dying to self and surrendering of control so we are left with nothing to hold to but Him. Stillness is humility and trust. It is allowing Him to be our all in all, which requires anything not of Him to take a backseat, including our selves. Everything about us—from our individual characteristics that give us distinction to the base-level simplicity of our humanity—will and must come into submission to the reality of Him. "Be still, and know I am God,"[2] eternally resounds throughout the earth, and the Lord will not change the subject. Stillness is a prerequisite for *knowing* Him. It must be.

Being still requires a "letting go," especially of control. When we let go of control in all its forms—our plans, the busyness that gives us counterfeit significance, and the 24/7 noise we use to suppress the silence we are afraid to face—the Lord Himself fills the void, a most wonderful exchange. But stillness takes courage, endurance, and faith, for it goes against how we have been conditioned by the world. In stillness, initially our flesh will surely throw a fit, and the silence will bring us face to face with every unholy, anxious thought that has occupied our minds. The waiting will sometimes feel like a free fall, but that is faith, and each trust lean gets easier as we learn His ways. He *always* shows up—He is the Faithful One. He promises to take care of all we strive to solve ourselves if we only seek Him first.[3]

---

[2] Psalm 46:10
[3] Matthew 6:33

Remember that He is *near*, closer than our skin, more powerful than our minds can comprehend. And He is kind. The command to "be still" is not a belittling of our problems or pain, but the compassionate appeal of the One, in Whose Spirit resides our only true peace and comfort. Anxiety need not rule us any longer. The Peace that transcends understanding, Jesus Himself[4], will guard our hearts and minds if we simply present our problems to Him in prayer and then turn our attention to Him instead.[5] Give up control. Trust God. Mind renewal begins in that about-face in thinking, our knowledge of Him growing deeper as we accept His invitation to rest.

***

Rest is our inheritance as redeemed sons and daughters of God, paid for us by Jesus Christ on the cross. It is finished[6]; He accomplished it all, freeing us from the very religious spirit that continually prompts us to "do" to secure our salvation. We must not be deceived—His blood was and forever will be enough to save us. Religion stands at arms length and shouts, *"Strive!"* But our Redeemer leans in and whispers, *"Abide."* It is the invitation, the whisper, we are after. His whisper is everything. A religious mindset assumes striving is required, but stillness has the humility to restfully wait for the whisper.

Rest is a byproduct of stillness, because stillness of soul is what enables us to begin making withdraws on our inheritance of rest. An inheritance of rest, accessed through stillness, includes more than just peace in

---

[4] Ephesians 2:14
[5] Philippians 4:5-7
[6] John 19:30

adverse situations. While God cares about our needs, He is interested in a higher reality. The revelation that we can rest because He will meet all of our needs and that we are unconditionally loved, not needing to work for it, frees us up. We are free to raise our gaze from His mighty hand of power and provision to finally become fixated on His face. Rest reveals Him further. And when we have tasted and seen[7] His divine nature, when we have looked into those eyes of fire[8] for ourselves, we realize how beautiful, how irresistible our King is. Hunger for greater knowledge of Him starts there. Abiding begins in that place.

Mary Magdalene understood this. She sat at the Lord's feet listening to Him speak. As in our own lives, there was pressure for her to be distracted by tasks and worry was waiting for an open door within her. But she chose stillness. She chose resting at the Master's feet, and Jesus commended her for choosing the one, better thing[9]. It was Him; He was the only thing she needed in that moment. And she—her nearness, attention, and surrender—was what He delighted in and desired, as well.

Intimacy with God is so simple that we can overlook it. We often miss its power and the fact that it is *everything*. We were created for intimacy with Him, to know Him and be known by Him. The world cannot comprehend the level of intimate communion with God available in the Gospel, because the world defines success differently; it looks at the simplicity of stillness, that restful abiding at Jesus' feet, and declares, "There must be more to it!" But there isn't. The abiding lifestyle Mary

---

[7] Psalm 34:8
[8] Revelation 1:14
[9] Luke 10:38-42

chose is downright offensive to those who are looking for steps to success, principles that lead to blessing. They hope to bypass the abiding and get right to the fruit— idolizing the increase, not willing to surrender, they want to overstep relationship with the Father, all the while demanding His inheritance. This is the way of the world, the natural mindset that cannot understand the things of God.[10]

But thankfully, when we are born again, we receive the mind of Christ,[11] and Holy Spirit helps us break off the world's pattern of thought. When we let Him govern our minds, He transforms us and aligns our thinking with His, bringing us life and peace.[12] As we continue to let go through stillness the easier abiding in Christ becomes. A heart posture like Mary's can be our norm, making us a people who treasure His Presence, and paradoxically we will accomplish greater things for God from that restful place than those who never stop striving. It is one of many Kingdom conundrums.

***

Stillness and abiding are almost synonymous. Both require surrender, rest, and complete dependence on our Life Source. Jesus teaches in John's Gospel that He is the True Vine, and we are the branches.[13] He says abiding in Him and allowing His words to abide in us are what make us fruitful[14]—it is how we have life. We need to grasp the significance of this two-part instruction.

---

[10] 1 Corinthians 2:14
[11] 1 Corinthians 2:16
[12] Romans 8:6, 12:2
[13] John 15:1, 5
[14] John 15:5-8

Valuing His words is integral in our connection with the Vine. Like Mary, we actually need to be still and *listen* to Him. Listening in stillness honors God and reveals our value for His voice, because it creates space for Him to speak. It is where we step down from the stage, taking our reason, plans, and opinions with us—a concession that His ways, thoughts, and words are higher.[15]

He longs to speak to us. More precisely, He wants us to hear Him, for He is *always* speaking. We need simply to make a practice of stilling ourselves throughout our days—pausing in His Presence, acknowledging His nearness, and asking Holy Spirit, "What is on Your mind, God?" And just as we need humility to let God speak, we must be humble enough to allow God to speak however He sees fit. The Spirit's language has a complexity broader than any human language, and it takes intimacy to discern how He is speaking in any given moment. He speaks through Scripture, through His Spirit directly to our spirits ("the whisper"), through dreams, through the people around us, and countless other ways. Developing our consciousness to the language of Holy Spirit is a lifelong adventure—an adventure simultaneously fulfilling and overwhelming. The God of the universe speaks to us! Most wonderful of all, Jesus is the Word[16], so when God shares His words with us, He is sharing Himself. He reveals His nature to us through His words—they are an overflow of His heart.[17] Even *how* God speaks tells us about Who He is, if we are willing to press into His ways.

For the hungry ones, those who long know Him and value His words, there must be a willingness to pay the

---

[15] Isaiah 55:9

[16] John 1:1, 14

[17] Matthew 12:34

price of stillness. Again, stillness requires surrender. It requires silence. Surrendering to silence is countercultural, inevitably being uncomfortable at first. All we have avoided arises in silence—anxieties, past pains, and inconsequential idols. Those things are real, but the greater Truth also resides there. He comes in gently, bringing balms for past hurts, comfort for grief, and peace to our instabilities. His words have that power. The whole of His creation responds to His voice. We must remember how raging waves and wind instantly calmed at the Lord's "Peace! Be still!"[18] What if we let Him make the same declaration within us? His words are filled with grace[19] and creative power,[20] so surely the storms within us would also cease.

***

Creation itself proclaims the nature of God. In His kindness, God has embroidered our world with reminders of what is possible for the abiding believer. But while those reminders of His eternal power and divine nature (what can be known about God) should be clearly seen,[21] they can be missed if we stay self-absorbed. "Consider the wildflowers"[22] was not a pet suggestion, intended to simply sound poetic or useful for an inspirational catchphrase—it was a command. "Considering" requires us to look outside ourselves, to redirect our thoughts from our problems, and to focus on the truths of His nature being revealed through His

---

[18] Mark 4:39
[19] Luke 4:22
[20] Psalm 33:8
[21] Romans 1:19-20
[22] Luke 12:27

handiwork. Wildflowers, simple, fragile, helpless, yet beautiful, reveal God as the Loving Provider Who cares about the small details. The Father knows our needs. Oceans proclaim His fierce passion, displaying His raw power and the depths of His love and mercy.[23] Starry skies reveal His glory and the infinite, expansive knowledge of God[24] that we will never be able to scratch the surface of—an awesome testament to the Holy One Who beckons us closer despite our humanity.

This kind of considering, the attentive observation of creation and meditation on what is learned about Him in the process, is what led David to pen: *"What is mankind that God is mindful of them?"* Consideration in stillness gave him proper perspective. He was humbled by Who God is, and in the revelation of God, he also received further revelation of the honor, glory, and authority the Father has bestowed upon us.[25] A pure understanding of our own greatness, one untainted by pride, can only come in the context of God.

***

Continual consideration of His nature and prayerful mediation on His Word tear down longstanding strongholds in our thinking.[26] As those strongholds are demolished, they are replaced by our revelations of Him. They take root to the point that Truth becomes unquestionable within us. Faith is then our first response when problems come, rather than an afterthought when anxiety has already taken its toll. Stillness becomes the

---

[23] Micah 7:19
[24] Psalm 19:1-2
[25] Psalm 8:3-8
[26] 1 Corinthians 10:4-5

state we long to dwell in, because He is there—it becomes our lifestyle, as we grow deeper and deeper in the knowledge of Him. Surrender is no longer something we dread, because we have learned His ways; we know and trust He will give us more of Him the more of ourselves we lose.

The Lord wants to bring His Church into that level of surrendered maturity. He wants a Church that highly values stillness—a Body of believers who, like Elijah, wont be fooled by hype, noise, and spectacle if He is not in it. He wants us to lean in for the still, small whisper,[27] not settling until He speaks. Unprecedented power is available within His whisper for those who listen.

Above that, though, Holy Spirit searches for a people who are willing to simply be still in the silence and know Him. The ability to sit silently with someone and enjoy their company without words is a sign of deep relational intimacy. It is the same in our relationship with Jesus. Stillness before Him forms the foundation for friendship with God and healthy fear of the Lord.

---

[27] 1 Kings 19:11-13

CHAPTER FOUR:
FEAR OF THE LORD

The Lord is found in stillness. As we spend intentional time with Him there, a renovation begins inside us. We start to fear the Lord. This type of fear should not to be confused with shame, a fear from the flesh that compels us to hide from Him, to detach from holy connection, like in the garden after the Fall.[1] Fear of the Lord draws us *to* Him, shepherding us into a more full knowledge of His nature. The fire within that holds us to unbending, zealous pursuit of God, fear of the Lord sets us apart from the world. Finding Him forces a decision. When we know what He is like, we can no longer live or think in ways that are contrary to Who He has revealed Himself to be. We are held accountable, because we have tasted and seen His nature for ourselves.[2] What we partake of in that secret place of still fixation on Him is both delightful and terrifying, and we come to realize how "other" the Lord is. He is not like us.

Sometimes our own humanity skews and limits our perception of God. He cannot be enclosed in small perceptions; they shatter when we get even the tiniest glimpse of Who He is. Outside of time, our Alpha and Omega[3] is so "other"—so magnificent, omniscient, omnipotent, holy, just, and beyond words in every way. He is the Life Source, the Light,[4] the Glorious Father.[5]

---

[1] Genesis 3:8

[2] Psalm 34:8

[3] Revelation 1:8

[4] John 8:12

God created us in His image,[6] but we must be careful not to conform Him to ours by incorrect thinking. His thoughts and ways are not ours: they are higher.[7] Yet the Lord reveals His higher ways and thoughts, not to create distance or to tauntingly belittle us, but to restore the standard and increase intimacy. Jesus is the Standard to Whom we must conform. He reveals what He is like to show us what we are to attain to as image bearers of the King, mercifully inviting us to seek Him since He is near and to forsake our low, wicked ways.[8]

We often miss God's invitation, because we find the infinitude of God intimidating (which it should be) and we deem true relationship with Him an impossible endeavor; thus we miss out on growing in the knowledge of Him. But as we go higher,[9] setting our minds on His thoughts and ways,[10] we are conformed by Holy Spirit into the image of Christ,[11] clothing ourselves in His nature[12] to the extent that Who He is shines through us. That kind of covenant connection, that holiness, enables us to see the Lord with greater clarity,[13] as He uncovers layer after layer of His heart. Those who fear the Lord spend their lives answering that call to holiness:[14] aligning their thinking with the truth of Who He is and

---

[5] Ephesians 1:17
[6] Genesis 1:26
[7] Isaiah 55:8-9
[8] Isaiah 55:6-7
[9] Revelation 4:1
[10] Colossians 3:2
[11] 2 Corinthians 3:18; 1 Corinthians 15:49; Romans 8:29
[12] Colossians 3:12; Romans 13:14; Galatians 3:27
[13] Hebrews 12:14
[14] 2 Corinthians 7:1

who they are, pursuing intimacy with Jesus at all costs, and allowing His words to sanctify them.[15]

***

Fearing God is loving Him, and meeting Love[16] on a relational level changes everything. Religious duty and rituals are foreign words to the lovesick, for the revelation of His nature as Love (not to mention all His other qualities) captivates. Jesus is irresistible—He is the desire of every heart, in every nation[17]—falling in love with Him becomes inevitable when we see His beauty. Receptive recognition of His love enables us to love Him back.[18] Loving Him is the fruit of knowing Him.[19]

If we have fallen in love with Him, our values shift. Our sole desire becomes dwelling within His nearness in restful stillness, living out the endless cycle of gazing on His beauty before us and relentlessly seeking after the more of Him yet to be found.[20] We then stop skirting the lines, looking to see how much we can get away with and still remain in God's good graces; instead, because we have shifted from servants to lovers, we long to know what pleases Him.[21] His delight becomes our delight, His disappointment our despair. We fear the day we do anything outside of His initiation and grieve His Spirit.[22] His Presence becomes supreme.

---

[15] John 15:3
[16] 1 John 4:8
[17] Haggai 2:7
[18] 1 John 4:19
[19] 1 John 4:7
[20] Psalm 27:4
[21] Ephesians 5:10
[22] Ephesians 4:30

As we grow in love for Him and fear of Him, we begin to value His Word—His will and nature are found there. The Bible reveals the Father's heart, and points us towards one Person, Jesus. What He has said and what He is saying need to be the constant tethers we never outgrow. Like the psalmist who wrote Psalm 119, longing for more God's words can consume us[23] if we posture ourselves properly, if we fear the Lord and value what He says above any other voice.

An increased desire to read Scripture comes partially by asking God to give us a hunger for His Word and inviting Holy Spirit to teach us; however, a portion falls on us. We are to approach the Word with diligence, discipline, and intentionality—trusting Him to reveal Himself on the pages and allowing the sword of the Spirit to cut deep wherever necessary.[24] Making His words a priority creates a snowball effect in our lives. Loving Him becomes our natural response, spending time with Him our genuine desire, because *He* has become our Treasure. Our hearts always follow what we willfully choose to treasure.[25]

Jesus is the Truth we are to give everything for and never sell.[26] Following Him costs us but He is a more than worthy investment. And He gave everything to have us when He died on the cross—what other response besides complete surrender is there? When He takes the first place in our hearts, over any promise we have been given or anything we want Him to do for us, true peace

---

[23] Psalm 119:20, 40
[24] Hebrews 4: 12; Ephesians 6:17
[25] Matthew 6:21
[26] Proverbs 23:23

and joy and fulfillment finally manifest in our lives. It is what "seeking first the Kingdom"[27] looks like.

***

In God's Kingdom, we grow in hunger the more we eat the Bread of Life,[28] living off every word He speaks.[29] It is the daily bread we are to live dependent upon[30]—a dependency intrinsic to fear of the Lord that recognizes only His words give life and knowing Him is only possible by His direct revelation.[31] That fearful dependency kills fear of man and silences any stranger's voice.[32] It is impossible to care about people's opinions when our minds are so renewed we actually believe what He says.

Who He has revealed Himself to be can become an unshakable reality within us, a trust that flows from meditation on what He says about Himself and then having those revelations of His nature confirmed by experience. Choosing to listen to His voice and meditate on what He says, even before we have noticed Who He is in our personal experience, increases our awareness and changes the lens through which we view life. It is all a part of faith, a key to abiding in Him, and how we come to find Him everywhere. Persecution and challenges inevitably come against us when we become that aware of Him; worldly minds consider things of Holy Spirit foolishness.[33] But those who humbly cling to the Father

---

[27] Matthew 6:33

[28] John 6:48

[29] Matthew 4:4

[30] Matthew 6:11

[31] John 14:21

[32] John 10:5

[33] 1 Corinthians 2:12-16

and avoid the fear-of-man-rooted pride of life[34] will be entrusted with more of God than they could ever imagine.

***

Humility is fear of the Lord,[35] and the fear of the Lord is the beginning of wisdom.[36] Coming in low before God with reverence and worship attests that we are beginning to see God for Who He is. The humble are far too hungry for more of Him and too aware of their complete dependency on Him to let pride get in the way. Fear of the Lord established in humility attracts wisdom, for it proves to God that He can trust us. Those who fear Him have no agendas but pleasing, serving, loving, and knowing Him more; therefore, there is room within them for God to build something wonderful—He can lay a foundation for wisdom to rest upon.

Everyone longs for wisdom, whether they realize it or not, for within it lies life strategies from heaven and the secrets of God's heart. Priceless and precious,[37] wisdom leads to an enriched life and favor with the Lord.[38] Because of its power, God only entrusts it to the humble, king-hearted ones who fear Him—to give it to the foolish or prideful would be wasteful and dangerous, like throwing pearls to pigs.[39] He will not give wisdom to people who lack the maturity to steward it responsibly, for their sake and the sake of those around them. But He

---

[34] 1 John 2:15-17
[35] Proverbs 22:4
[36] Proverbs 9:10
[37] Proverbs 8:11
[38] Proverbs 8:35
[39] Matthew 7:6

confides in us when fear Him, broadening our understanding of the love covenant we share[40] and entrusting more of Himself to us. Jesus Himself is Wisdom,[41] so anytime we grow in wisdom, we are growing in the knowledge of Christ. Seeking wisdom only increases our ability to fear Him and know Him,[42] which protects us from idols that try to seduce us out of covenant with our First Love.[43] It locks us into Love, and empowers us to fulfill His will.

***

The Lord is not interested in simply making us smarter or giving us more information. Just as knowing Him trumps knowing about Him, the words and revelations we receive from Him as a result of fearing Him lead unto something greater than mere head knowledge. A response is required of us. Fearing the Lord consists of both doing what He says and believing what He says. If fearing the Lord means loving the Lord, then we need to do what He asks of us—Jesus taught that our obedience to His commands demonstrates our love for Him.[44] If we do not follow through with what is asked of us, then we do not love Him and cannot claim to know Him.[45] What He asks of us can be found in His Word and taught to us by Holy Spirit. Swift and thorough obedience gives us access to the grace available

---

40 Psalm 25:14

41 1 Corinthians 1:30

42 Proverbs 2:5

43 Proverbs 2:12-22; Revelation 2:4

44 John 14:15

45 1 John 2:3-6

to complete our assignments.[46] We must avoid lukewarm complacency at all costs.

The lukewarm life is the fallout of being spread too thin with our affections, our fear, and our worship. Complacent hearts repulse the Lord.[47] He wants nothing to do with a lifestyle that suggests He should share the throne with other gods and other voices. Jesus is either everything to us or He is nothing to us. He is God, and there is no other.[48] No other Name. No other King. No other Way.

Almost always, the idols we need to dethrone reign in our beliefs, not only our beliefs about God but also our beliefs about ourselves. If we fear Him, we will believe what He says about us, even when it is costly. Will we still abide when He gives us a holy confidence— a confidence that requires a shedding of false humility and often offends the insecure, costing us praises from men? Are we willing to be misunderstood to embrace Truth? No matter how costly sticking to Truth is, not allowing Holy Spirit to change us proves far more costly—it is simply perilous to take His words as suggestions instead of commands. The root of such a response is pride, because we assume we know better than the Lord, and God openly opposes such people.[49] To be in such standing with God is more terrifying than any attack of the devil.

But if we keep our eyes single-focused on Jesus[50] and resist the instability caused by double-minded unbelief,[51]

---

[46] Hebrews 4:16

[47] Revelation 3:16

[48] Deuteronomy 4:35

[49] Proverbs 3:34

[50] Hebrews 12:2

[51] James 5-8

we will receive ever-increasing measures of wisdom and profound revelations of God's nature. His perfect love will cast out any unholy fear from our hearts.[52] Healthy fear of the Lord keeps us connected to the Vine. It conforms us to His image, synchronizing our hearts until we love what He loves[53] and hate what He hates.[54] A people who fear Him are unshakable lovers of God.

The Lord calls us to be such a people, in this day and hour, especially. If we answer the call, we will possess food the world knows nothing about[55]—the praises of man will not sustain us, nor will the world's criticism crush us. We will once again tremble at His voice alone,[56] and what a great trembling that will be! As a result, the Lord can trust us with the invitation to ascend the Mountain, shrouded in the mysterious cloud of His Presence, where character is built and His ways are discovered.

---

[52] 1 John 4:18
[53] Psalm 118:4
[54] Proverbs 8:13
[55] John 4:32
[56] Psalm 119:162

CHAPTER FIVE:
MOUNTAIN OF MYSTERY

When fear of the Lord becomes our motivator for life, when it takes root on a near DNA level, our hunger for God intensifies. He becomes our obsession—the One ever on our minds, the voice we cannot live without. We will do anything for more, emboldened to pursue by the glimpses of His majesty He has graced us with. That abandonment of heart towards the Lord opens us up to the subtle beckoning of the Master. He invites us to ascend His mountain of mystery. His mystery is the mountain we must climb, because everything about God is mysterious. If we believe we have Him figured out, we have been deceived into creating a god in our own image.

Every component of our Christian lives—our born-again experiences where Christ comes to dwell within us,[1] the baptism and infillings of the Holy Spirit,[2] the Bible unlocked for us by the Spirit as Teacher,[3] gifts of the Spirit, like tongues,[4] God's incomprehensible grace that sustains and saves us[5]—emanates mystery. In fact, Jesus Himself is the Mystery of God.[6] We must learn to embrace God's mystery or we do not truly embrace Jesus. While knowing God in His entirety remains

---

[1] Colossians 1:27; John 3:3-9
[2] Acts 2:2; Ephesians 4:18
[3] 1 Corinthians 2:10-12
[4] 1 Corinthians 14:2
[5] Ephesians 2:8
[6] Colossians 2:2

impossible, He still welcomes us to come higher, to learn more about Him. The more we learn about God, the more we realize how much we do not know. If that mysterious side of Him frustrates us and we shy away from it for the sake of our own understanding, we miss a beautiful opportunity to die to ourselves. We choose the point where we level off in our growth in the knowledge of God.

His mystery cannot become an excuse for apathy. It is our glory,[7] our inheritance,[8] our *privilege* to seek out the deep things of God—the treasure trove of wisdom and knowledge hidden in Christ.[9] God freely gives us the knowledge of the secrets of His Kingdom; therefore, ascending that mountain of mystery is not just the only logical response but also good stewardship of what He has already revealed to us.[10] Climbing the mountain is our noble love quest, where we are spurred on, not by striving, but a grateful response to His lavish grace. It is our joy and delight to ascend, because we know it pleases Him. For facing mystery head-on requires faith and trust—how we step out of the realm of the flesh[11] and demonstrate belief when He says He rewards those who seek Him.[12]

The Lord's mystery empowers us to pursue; it is both the why and the how of the climb. It awakens our inner child: reverential wonder due God for what He has revealed and the trustful curiosity needed to seek after what is yet hidden. Childlikeness itself is a mystery—it is

---

[7] Proverbs 25:2
[8] Deuteronomy 29:29
[9] Colossians 2:3
[10] Matthew 13:11
[11] Romans 8:8
[12] Hebrews 11:6

the only way we are given access to the revelations of God available on the mountain. Unless we become like a child, wholly dependent on the Father with adoration and devotion, we will miss out on the perpetual novelty of simply enjoying Him. A mind "enlightened" by the world's wisdom has lost its ability to interact with the Lord in that way.

***

For those who require an intellectual grasping before they open their hearts to believing God, offense roadblocks every turn; His mystery is *filled* with tension, which always frustrates human understanding. The childlike mind of Christ[13] must be renewed within us if we are to ascend the mountain. It pleases the Father to reveal more of Himself to those who are like little children, while hiding the same revelation from those who are not,[14] because child-hearted ones will survive mystery's tension.

Tension is a necessary part of growing in the knowledge of God and the ultimate test of our belief in Who He has revealed Himself to be. We feel the discomfort almost immediately after we choose to become a follower of Jesus and desire to know God relationally. While He is Truth, that Truth is unbending and often goes directly against how we have been taught to think. The Kingdom overflows with paradoxes (we must lose our lives to live[15] and our greatness comes through lowly, childlike servanthood),[16] and the

---

[13] 1 Corinthians 2:16
[14] Matthew 11:25-27
[15] Luke 9:23-24
[16] Matthew 20:25-28; Matthew 18:1-5

Scriptures are filled with tension. For example, Jesus did not heal the same way every time, but then commands us to follow His example of healing the sick, without any further instructions on *how*.[17] He told one rich man to give all his money to the poor,[18] while not requiring the same of every wealthy friend or follower He had, like Joseph of Arimathea[19] or Lazarus, Martha, and Mary.[20] The paradoxical tension is intentional. Relationship with Him resides at its core.

Jesus modeled how to navigate tension through His relational reliance on the Father, doing only what He saw His Father do[21] and only saying what He heard His Father say.[22] That combination of living by "daily bread"[23]—reliance on the Father's voice in the present—and active obedience to His instruction propels us up the mountain into greater knowledge of Him. It is how we remain connected to the Father's heart.

Resisting the tension means resisting relationship. There are two alternatives to tension: We either turn principles learned from past experiences into rigid rules, which leads to cold, legalistic religion. Or we chalk up everything to the sovereignty of God, which fosters complacency in our hearts and distorts our perceptions of His goodness and our identities as His children. Both ways stand in opposition to intimacy with God and testify to our ungodly impulses to be in control and to fit God in a box the size of our comprehension. Life with God consists of pressing in and letting go. Which one

---

[17] Matthew 10:8

[18] Luke 18:22

[19] Matthew 27:57

[20] John 12:1-8

[21] John 5:19

[22] John 12:49

[23] Matthew 6:11; John 4:4

should we do in any given moment? Relationship is how we know—listening to Holy Spirit's voice, growing in the knowledge of His ways, and daily internalization of His Word.

Mystery's tension also checks our motives, and reveals just how anchored we are in His nature. Are we truly in it for Him? Or do we seek to know Him for what He can do for us? Because He is kind, He does not despise the desire for blessing, but He shares His secrets and subtleties with those who have no other agenda except knowing Him intimately. Stepping into His mystery, ascending that mountain, puts our hearts to the test. If we experience tragedies, setbacks, or disappointments, do we still believe He is good? If He instructs us to do something challenging that offends our minds—like Jesus telling the crowds to "eat His flesh and drink His blood"[24]—without any further explanation or clarification, will we still step out obediently and trust Him? In those moments, we learn if our beliefs about His nature are circumstantially based or if they are connected to the steadfast reality of Who He is as God Almighty.

The hard truth is: the nature of God is not dependent upon our comfort. It is not even dependent upon our perceptions of past experiences. He is good because He says He is. We must start there. In choosing to believe what He says about Himself—pushing past disappointment and offense and going into His Presence—we learn Who He is by intimate experience. Those heart revelations of His nature, those encounters with Him, become unshakable anchor points within us. When we have experienced His goodness, kindness, mercy, you name it, circumstances have less power to

---

[24] John 6:35-58

send us reeling. We are able to trust He turns all things around for our good,[25] knowing He is more real and unwavering than our adverse circumstances appear to be. We begin to see His nature in everything when He becomes our Prize—the Lover our eyes look for in every crowd, every situation.

Knowing Him experientially from the heart, without the prerequisite of mental understanding, frees us from the why's of life the enemy often uses to create distance between us and God. Even in the mysteries of life and God, His goodness (or any other aspect of His nature) can become unquestionable within us. Abiding in His words and growing in constant awareness of His nearness tethers us to Him in hope.[26] Mystery remains, seasons change, yet our connection with Him stays unscathed. We begin to love His mysterious side, no longer wanting to pick and choose which aspects of His nature increase our own comfort. Embracing God's mystery, tension and all, is integral to knowing Him more and vital to maturing as surrendered children of God. Character is built in that beautiful tension.

***

Much like stillness of soul, "ascending the mountain of mystery" is more a heart posture than a physical act. It is a lifestyle of sanctified stillness before Him and daily, disciplined pursuit of His voice, even when we face disappointment or lack understanding. The halfhearted do not survive the climb. Ascension makes us vulnerable to the elements of life, for we can take less with us the higher we go and the longer we stay there. The idols in

---

[25] Romans 8:28
[26] Hebrews 6:19; Hebrews 10:23

which we have placed false security are the price we must pay. Those things are deadweight when we are learning to live a life of faith.

If we cut out control and face our fear head-on, we find just how fulfilling the Lord can be.[27] Within the tension of surrendered dependency, the Faithful One demonstrates how He will never fail us.[28] The rewards of His Presence and provision are worth what the mountain requires of us, no matter how costly, challenging, and perilous the climb.

Yet many find God's mystery off-putting and inconvenient; thus, the mountain is a lonely place where few ever go. But if we accept His invitation to ascend, we will find ourselves in the midst of good company. Friends of God spend their lives habitually seeking the Lord on the mountainside—people like Moses,[29] Elijah,[30] and countless others, past and present. Even Jesus,[31] during His life on earth, demonstrated what a mountainside lifestyle looks like. A place of prayer and communion, His friends find sanctuary there, and because they fear Him, they have learned by experience it is the safest place to be.

Lingering in the valley, living off of the spoils of past victories and the Lord's blessings, can be disastrous if we become complacent there. Sometimes comfort lulls us to sleep spiritually and dulls our hunger for Him. We must not be like the people of Israel in Moses' day. They distanced themselves when God spoke to them from the mountain, preferring to bypass direct intimacy and have

---

[27] Philippians 4:19; 2 Corinthians 9:8
[28] 2 Timothy 2:13; Isaiah 58:11
[29] Exodus 19:20
[30] 1 Kings 19:8
[31] Luke 6:12

Moses serve as the middleman between them and God instead.[32] As a result, a manmade idol took the Lord's place in their hearts.[33] The same can happen to us if we are content being spoon-fed by others, all of our revelation about the Lord coming secondhand. Jesus died so any space of separation between Him and us could vanish. How could we dishonor Him by not stepping into the holy place He has given us access to in this new covenant?[34]

***

While the Giver is infinitely more valuable than the gifts, the blessings of God in the valley are wonderful and worthy of thankful enjoyment. With the correct perspective, blessings can also be great starting points for pulling ourselves out of the valley if we have stayed there too long—purifying our hearts to a place of childlikeness[35] and reinstating pursuing Him as our top priority. For instance, the mystery bread, the "what is it?" manna, [36] the Lord fed the Israelites with in the wilderness testified to Jesus, the true Bread of Life and Mystery we are to live by.[37] Having mystery bread to eat every day should have inspired the people of God to humbly consider the nature of the One causing it to appear each morning. Every blessing or gift God gives reveals something about Him. Although He gives out of love, with no strings attached, His provisional blessings

---

[32] Exodus 20:18-19

[33] Exodus 32:1

[34] Hebrews 10:9, 12:22-29

[35] Psalm 24:3-4

[36] Exodus 16:15

[37] John 6:35

are covered with His fingerprints—He does not wish to remain anonymous, and He patiently waits to see if we will be wooed in to know Him more.

If we are content receiving God's blessing alone, we stop short of something marvelous. Jacob clung to the Lord to receive blessing, but did not press in past that point to apprehend God's name. Jacob asked God Who He was, but the Lord responded with a mysterious question: "Why do you ask My name?"[38] God does not lack information—His questions are always invitations and tests of our hearts.[39]

The life of Moses shows what is possible if someone chooses to press into that question and seek after His name. Moses bypassed the promised blessing of God[40] and clung to the Lord, imploring Him as a friend to stay. He recognized the heart-wrenching implications if God withdrew His Presence.[41] Because Moses faithfully valued the Presence on the mountain over the blessings in the valley and persistently stepped into the cloud of mystery,[42] God granted his requests and more, giving Him what Jacob asked for but did not receive: the Lord's name.[43]

God's nature is encapsulated in His name—it holds His promises, covenant, power and authority, our salvation,[44] and all His mystery. When we pray in the name of Jesus, we are holding Him to His word to act in accordance with His nature, for He swears by Himself.[45]

---

[38] Genesis 32:24-29

[39] Proverbs 17:3

[40] Exodus 33:1-3

[41] Exodus 33:15-16

[42] Exodus 20:21

[43] Exodus 33:19, 34:6-7

[44] Acts 4:12

[45] Isaiah 45:23

God sharing His nature-laced name with Moses was a sacred experience, only available to friends of God who spend time face-to-Face with Him on the mountain. Intentional time spent loving Him in His Presence, embracing His mystery and never limiting Him to our understanding, shows we finally value the Face of God above His Hand of provision, as marvelous as that is.

**

Gazing into the Lord's face changes ours—we become radiant, [46] our image conforming into His glorious image.[47] Allowing His face to shine upon us is a prerequisite for His name being placed upon us, [48] meaning the light of His face and the power of His name work in tandem to change us to look more like Christ. We always take on the nature of Who or what we worship.[49] Our mandate to represent Christ on the earth is not possible through our own striving, but through secluded intimacy on the mountain.

Over time and endurance built, the mountain becomes our refuge, ascending His mystery our never-ending enchantment. We find home on the mountain, because He is there; however, being hidden in God does not mean shutting the world out. What we gain on the mountaintop is unto something much greater than ourselves. From the revelation entrusted to us in that lofty place, we discover our divine purpose of priesthood unto the Lord.

---

[46] Psalm 34:5; Exodus 34:29
[47] 2 Corinthians 3:18
[48] Numbers 6:22-27
[49] Jeremiah 2:5

CHAPTER SIX:
PRIESTHOOD & EXPANSION

Friends of God who dwell on the mountain gain a perspective inaccessible anywhere else. In the light of the Lord's face, when His glory passes by, [1] we are enlightened [2] and entrusted with revelation—not only fresh revelation but also reminders of revelation received years ago that has been blunted in impact because of familiarity. God enabling us to experience Who He is and what He has done once again, as if it were the first time, testifies to His mercy. We remember the cross, how we were saved from sin, darkness, and despair by the blood of Beautiful King Jesus. We remember what resulted from His resurrection—an unbreakable union with Him that has elevated and seated us with Him, in Him, in heavenly places. [3]

An unveiling occurs in those moments of revelatory glory, and we see the disparity between what Truth says about us and what is commonly manifesting in our daily lives. Holy Spirit intends to firmly reestablish His nature as Lord and uproot idols (the sin and enemy's lies that have hindered our prayers [4] and shaped us into something less than God created us to be [5]) in our thinking. While the Light can be uncomfortable because it exposes our compromises, through it God illuminates

---

[1] Exodus 33:18-19

[2] Psalm 36:9

[3] Ephesians 2:6

[4] Isaiah 59:2

[5] Psalm 115:8; Jeremiah 2:5

His dreams for His temple. *We* are that temple,[6] and the plans He outlines give glimpses into what our secret place with Him should and can look like[7]—a shared life abounding in fulfilling communion and communication with God. If we know Him enough to discern the kind invitation within the revelation, repentance[8] and prayer will be our responses.

***

As we fall more in love with Him, any drift from the Standard will grieve us, because we know it grieves Him and hinders our sensitivity to His nearness and His will. But the grief need not be hopeless; rather a hunger for holiness can arise because the Lord has given us the ability to *repent*. Repentance is a willful turning from sin and an about-face in thinking. It is remorseful acknowledgement of our transgressions and a quick clinging to Him, allowing His love-words to remedy the effects of lies and accepting the forgiveness He freely gives. Repentance sustained—choosing Truth daily and swiftly realigning when He brings correction—leads to a renewed mind.

The repentant ones, set on being transformed by the Holy Spirit through mind renewal, [9] also become consumed with a passion for prayer. They have learned His nature, which has established a confident belief and trust in Who He says He is. That knowledge of Him produces a faith unafraid to make withdraws on His

---

[6] 2 Corinthians 6:16

[7] Ezekiel 43:4-12

[8] Romans 2:4

[9] Romans 12:2

promises through prayer—it is a trust that has the boldness to *ask* Him to do what He said He will do.

People of true prayer long for their First Love,[10] and they are willing to be the "amen" to God's desires to be found by His people[11] and to give His Spirit without measure.[12] They no longer pray their own prayers, but are praying the prayers of God; they listen, watch, and wait for His words and repeat them back to Him in prayer. This shift in the source of prayer shows a syncing of our hearts with the Lord's heart. His eyes ever rove the earth, searching for hearts that are completely and purely His,[13] a people He can lock eyes with. He calls us to be such a people—a royal, holy priesthood[14]—for priests are born of unrelenting repentance and prayer.

***

In our time, God is raising up a generation of Levites. These priests, these new Levites, have found their ultimate life's work: ministering to God and uncovering layer after layer of His heart. They are lovesick, consecrated, uncompromising, passionate, and courageous. They use the secret-place blueprints given to them on the mountain like treasure maps; they are on a quest to discover more of His ways (the reasons for His deeds, His subtleties, His personality). By giving careful attention to what the Lord reveals, they can recognize the entry doors to deeper realms of God and the exits out of

---

[10] Revelation 2:4
[11] Jeremiah 29:13
[12] John 3:34
[13] 2 Chronicles 16:9
[14] 1 Peter 2:9-10

intimacy to avoid.[15] Priests know by experience what pleases Him:[16] not token rituals[17] but a craving to know Him more[18] and circumcision of heart.[19]

God grants access into His sanctuary to those with circumcised hearts,[20] because they are willing to forsake any confidence they once had in carnal things[21] and be set apart to complete reliance on Him. They have locked eyes with Love in the temple of their soul, and the Consuming Fire they worshipfully[22] behold sets them ablaze—a fire they keep burning into eternity.[23] Levites are possessed by God. Worshipping Him and answering His heart cries are a priest's passionate compulsions.

If we accept the call to priesthood, we stand in proxy for our generation as both intercessors and prophetic messengers. We minister to Him through continuous prayer, a connection that becomes as natural as breathing. Because of the nearness required in such an ongoing dialogue, we are the first to respond when the Lord wonders, "Whom shall I send?"[24] The plans God whispers to us in our mountainside secret place must be proclaimed to the nations.[25] (Yet we still need the relational wisdom to know when to keep silent. Some revelations are for our individual ears only—God is a Friend and a Romantic like that.)

---

[15] Ezekiel 44:5
[16] Ephesians 5:10
[17] Psalm 51:16
[18] Hosea 6:6
[19] Deuteronomy 30:6; Psalm 51:17
[20] Ezekiel 44:7-9
[21] Philippians 3:3
[22] Hebrews 12:28-29; Revelation 1:14
[23] Leviticus 6:12-13
[24] Isaiah 6:8
[25] Matthew 10:27

Priesthood is not for the select few. The Lord, Who is no respecter of persons, [26] desires Levitical-level intimacy with all His children, regardless of their professions, social positions, or aptitudes. Therefore, priests are to reproduce themselves by relaying the Spirit's invitations and teaching others what it means to be holy[27] through their words and actions.

***

As modern-day, prophetic Levites, our lives are parables that indicate what the Lord intends to do in the Body at large. Societal reformation always begins with transformation and mind renewal within individuals. The Father is about to build something magnificent using His priests as living building stones.[28] To prepare us, He whispers to our spirits, *"Expand, expand, expand!"* Expansion is the season's theme and a prerequisite for revival.

God wants to expand our capacity to know Him—an increased experiential knowing, a saturation in His Spirit. He asks each of us to enlarge our tents, stretching them wide without restraint[29] beyond the borders of our own understanding and comfort. God is not unkind, nor is He wasteful; therefore He will not put something upon us that we lack the capacity or foundation to support. So it is important to expand in advance, preparing and purifying our hearts for the "more" God longs to release. Like the oil that flowed as long as the widow brought

---

[26] Acts 10:34-35
[27] Ezekiel 44:23
[28] 1 Peter 2:5
[29] Isaiah 54:2

jars,[30] what we receive from God in this imminent outpouring will be determined by our hunger and effort to expand.

We should expand with expectancy, rather than expectations. Expectations set limits on what we can receive from God, but expectancy invites infinite possibilities of fulfillment. It is all about embracing the mystery while remaining hopefully tethered to His nature as Promise Keeper. Jesus, Who already fills everything in every way,[31] will surely fill the space we create with richer revelations of His nature.

In the expansion period awaiting increase, priests find tension, similar to that found on the mountain of God's mystery. It is paramount that we press into the tension right away, for there can be no complacent slack in the holy tents He is erecting within us. Inevitably, temptations from the enemy creep in, endeavoring to cut our tent cords and fault our foundation through relapses into double-mindedness.[32] But His gracious, sufficient strength comes upon us in tension, no matter how weak we feel while fighting it.[33] Hungering for the more while remaining thankful for what He has already given are keys to staying in the sweet spot of God's will in a time of tension. Character, endurance, and capacity build as we embrace the tension in expansion.

Expansion of our internal "tents" so we can host more knowledge of His glory is an aspect of Kingdom advancement, and we must remember God's Kingdom advancement remains the great war of our time. Since

---

[30] 2 Kings 4:1-7
[31] Ephesians 1:23
[32] James 1:18
[33] 2 Corinthians 12:9

we are on the side of the Victorious One,[34] staying offensive on the frontlines of battle is the safest place for us to be—we cannot be lulled onto passive rooftops by the enemy like David before his downfall.[35]

The primary battleground in this holy war resides within the human mind, and we are commissioned by God to retake ground for the Kingdom there with violent tenacity.[36] It is imperative we put evil belief systems to death and tear down thought strongholds[37] the enemy has encamped in for far too long. Revelations of God's nature are the tent pegs that hold our expanded tents in place. Our tent pegs of truth are not only markers for Kingdom territory, but can also be the very weapons we use to slay unholy thoughts. As where Jael impaled her enemy with a tent peg[38] and where David hit Goliath with the stone,[39] God's truth must penetrate our temples—both our places of thought and our hearts' places of worship.

Lies we put to death will never revive if we continue establishing a purified Temple and plow new paths in our thinking. Hope must replace anxiety, love bitterness, and faith doubt. These new paths, or "ruts" in our thinking, are created through repetitive meditation on His nature. Too often we allow our minds to control us, placing no regulation on our meditation; thus we live in perpetual reaction and submission to whatever passes through our heads. Demonic strongholds are the byproduct of such negligence. But we can establish

---

[34] 1 Corinthians 15:57-58

[35] 2 Samuel 11:1-2

[36] Matthew 11:12

[37] 2 Corinthians 10:4-5

[38] Judges 4:21

[39] 1 Samuel 17:49

heavenly strongholds, centered on the nature of Jesus, if we partner with Holy Spirit and take authority over our thoughts.

Authority over our thoughts can be retaken through willful internalization of God's Word, practicing an awareness of Holy Spirit's nearness through stillness, and a lifestyle of worship centered in Who He is, not what He can do for us or the problems we want fixed. For priests such things are simply part of their delightful intimacy with and ministry to the Lord; however, in the spirit realm, that meditation is militant, a way we take the Kingdom and expand its borders by force.[40] It is what fixing our thoughts on Jesus[41] and taking every thought for Christ[42] looks like. A practical piece of tent-peg expansion, mind renewal is the reformation that ushers in His outpouring and instills the matured capacity within us to receive our inheritance.

***

God is the inheritance of His priests.[43] A mystery wonderful beyond words, we are not only the Lord's special possession,[44] but He is ours.[45] He entrusts us with more of Himself than we could ever dream when we sanctify ourselves through surrendered expansion. His Spirit of wisdom and revelation rushes in, filling the

---

[40] Matthew 11:12

[41] Hebrews 3:1

[42] 2 Corinthians 10:5

[43] Ezekiel 44:28

[44] 1 Peter 2:9

[45] Ezekiel 44:28

expectant space we have created with intimate, long-hidden knowledge of Him.[46]

Priests are forerunners, releasing the aroma of the knowledge of Him into the atmosphere,[47] for the smell of the Most Holy Place's fire ever lingers on them. The stewardship of their own revelation of His nature will lead to God entrusting them with entire people groups to teach about Him.[48] Soon the whole Body will be enticed by the aroma and follow suit into deeper knowledge of His nature. A corporate expansion and revival happens then. When we finally fully respond to our destinies as priests bound to minister to Him [49] and agents of expansion, the Body will come into a place of health, becoming a people distinguished by His Presence,[50] finally forming the house of prayer He has longed for.[51]

---

[46] Ephesians 1:17
[47] 2 Corinthians 2:14
[48] Luke 19:17
[49] Isaiah 56:6
[50] Exodus 33:15-16
[51] Isaiah 56:7

CHAPTER SEVEN:
EXPLOITS

Ever-increasing knowledge of the Lord's nature establishes a foundation for effective prayer and Kingdom exploits—it is how we individually and collectively are built into a house of prayer, where God dwells by Holy Spirit.[1] Each stone in the walls of that house is a memorial stone, commemorating marking moments of Divine revelation, declaring our history with God into future generations. And Jesus Christ forever remains the Cornerstone[2] all other stones rest upon. His nature is the love we are rooted and grounded in[3]—the Rock that gives us both intimate sanctuary and elevated perspective.[4] Prayer is the central, defining function of His house, because prayer is the natural outflow of intimacy. It is conversation in communion, an eternal love-exchange between us and the Lord.

When we as priests remain in an abiding dialogue with the Lord, never compartmentalizing ourselves out of the secret place, trust is nurtured. We begin to trust God to the point where His nature solidifies within our spirits, fostering an uncompromising faith in Him, and He expresses His trust in us by deepening the infusion of His heart and ours. We start seeing through the eyes of Truth,[5] becoming aware of the unholy state of the

---

[1] Ephesians 2:21-22
[2] Ephesians 2:20; 1 Corinthians 3:11
[3] Ephesians 3:17
[4] Psalm 18:2
[5] John 14:6

nations and the lostness of precious souls who do not yet know the Lord. God releases this honest diagnosis of humanity, not so we will distance ourselves and wash our hands of the world, but so we will infiltrate it with the Solution. God scours the earth for those who will humbly seek His face, pray for healing in their land,[6] and stand in the gap as intercessory representatives of repentance.[7] He is fiercely passionate about His stray sheep. The Father wants them all brought home.

The brokenness around us can no longer be seen as an inevitable judgment pronounced over the "others"—the ship we complacently watch sink from our lifeboats as we wait for Jesus to return and rescue us. We cannot put blame on God or even give too much credit to the devil: God commissioned us to be salt and light,[8] equipping us with all His power and authority[9] through Holy Spirit to live like Jesus in this world.[10] As the Father sent Jesus, we are sent out as ministers of reconciliation to reunite the Father with His children.[11] The Lord commits (not suggests) such a mandate to His whole household, and we must redeem the times [12] by responding quickly.

***

Priest-hearted people who know their God by experience will display supernatural strength and take

---

[6] 2 Chronicles 7:14

[7] Ezekiel 22:30

[8] Matthew 5:13-16

[9] Luke 9:1; 10:19

[10] 1 John 4:17

[11] John 20:21; 2 Corinthians 5:18-20

[12] Ephesians 5:16

action[13] in the name of Love. They own their charge as empowered children of God, and cannot help but share their stories as redeemed ones.[14] If we are priests who love the Lord, we will live out what we hear Him ask of us,[15] for our follow-through verifies our knowledge of Him.[16] His words that abide in us are not meant to remain hidden and stagnate, but to bear fruit.

No word God speaks returns to Him void,[17] for His words are creative,[18] containing His nature and faith ignition fluid in each syllable.[19] His powerful words within us and the responsibility that accompanies each revelation of His nature spur us to action. The "action" taken by those who know the Lord is twofold: prayer without ceasing[20] alone on the mountainsides of our souls and proclamation of the Good News to the masses in the valleys—a marriage of *asking* and *doing*, which allows what is in us to flow out of us like rivers of living water.[21]

***

The more we come to know God and recognize His ways, the more we realize the power of the "ask." He is a Rewarder of those who seek Him,[22] openly inviting us to

---

[13] Daniel 11:32b
[14] Psalm 107:2
[15] James 1:22
[16] 1 John 2:3-6
[17] Isaiah 55:11
[18] Genesis 1
[19] Romans 10:17
[20] 1 Thessalonians 5:17
[21] John 7:38
[22] Hebrews 11:6

ask Him for things—for greater measures of His Spirit,[23] for wisdom,[24] for mysteries of His heart,[25] for the inheritance of nations,[26] etc.—because we remain in Him.[27] When we ask, we pull upon the nature of God, holding Him to His promises and Who He has revealed Himself to be.

The Lord is not a tightfisted Father. Our petitions do not inconvenience Him. He *longs* for us to ask Him, to partner with Him through prayer to see His Kingdom advance in the earth. If we seem to be lacking in any area of our lives, perhaps we simply have not asked the Lord.[28]

But while the asking is important, knowing what to ask for is even more vital. The prophetic purposes of God's heart are whispered within the walls of the house of prayer, only picked up by those who have fearfully stilled themselves enough to discern His whisper. We must remain entrenched in the present, resisting the urge to get stuck in the past or fantasize about the future. Only then will we recognize the significance of what is available in the "now" of God and decipher what the Lord is doing in our day.

The present "now" words of God are laden with grace, because God sufficiently equips us when we partner with Him in His present-day, new works.[29] Like the sons of Issachar, we need an awareness of the times we are in and what we are to do in response.[30] If we lack

---

[23] Luke 11:13

[24] James 1:5

[25] Jeremiah 33:3

[26] Psalm 2:8

[27] Romans 15:7

[28] James 4:2

[29] Isaiah 42:9, 18-19

[30] 1 Chronicles 12:32

that awareness, we either create formulaic principles out of past experiences with God, presuming nothing has changed, or we make impatient assumptions about His will, pursuing something God did not initiate. Remaining present in the "now" with God keeps us dependent upon His voice and aligns us with His will. Discerning the current season by the Spirit reveals what we are to ask for—showing what God meant when He said, "ask for rain in the time of rain."[31]

***

In this season of the "ask," we are living in a time of abundant grace and favor for evangelism. The Lord desires us to ask Him to send out workers for the plentiful soul harvest.[32] From that place of prayer for laborers, we who know and fear God will find our own hearts responding to the urgent call to be sent ones. For when we are in pure, surrendered union with Him, Christ's love compels us to share the Gospel with others.[33] We cannot help it—our mouths always speak what our hearts are full of.[34]

Evangelism is a byproduct of mind renewal and an expression of our love for the Lord. His Spirit fills us with His compassion. Compassion gives proper perspective on the person in front of us, elevating our spiritual eyes so we no longer view anyone from a worldly, surface-level point of view.[35] Like Christ, we are

---

[31] Zechariah 10:1
[32] Matthew 9:38
[33] 2 Corinthians 5:14
[34] Matthew 12:34
[35] 2 Corinthians 5:17

able to see how harassed and helpless the lost are.[36] We recognize they are perishing because they do not know the Lord,[37] just as we once were; thus, we are not put off by how pain and deception manifest through their actions. That compassionate perspective is unto something superior than mere understanding—it provokes us to move, directing us to come closer to the people before us so the One dwelling inside us can make connection with them. He wants to step into the story of their lives with His restoration love. We are living testimonies of this God-dream: He did the same within all of us. Humanity desperately needs the blood of Jesus and the message of the cross.

**

If we have come to know the ways of God, we begin to anticipate the Lord's will in any situation we face. God does not change,[38] so the Jesus Who healed all who came to Him[39] still heals today; the Holy Spirit Who revealed Himself as "Comforter"[40] to the disciples still encourages and strengthens the brokenhearted; the Father Who sent His Son to seek and save the lost[41] is still not willing that any of His wayward children should perish.[42] Once we are aware of His will, as His lovers and priests, we discover His heart cries reverberating down the halls of our own hearts—desire awakening to see the will of

---

[36] Matthew 9:36

[37] Hosea 4:6

[38] Malachi 3:6; Numbers 23:19

[39] Matthew 4:24

[40] John 14:26

[41] Luke 19:10

[42] Matthew 18:14; 2 Peter 3:9

heaven's King done here on earth. [43] It is our commissioned responsibility to be ambassadors,[44] sent out with His authority to share the Good News and do Kingdom exploits.[45] What an honor.

Of course, preaching the Gospel of salvation, freeing the oppressed, and healing the sick are impossible in our own strength; yet God, in His mysterious love of partnership with us, wants us to be the vessels His power flows through. God is ever kind, and He is not setting us up for failure by giving us an impossible assignment. Our being "sent out" is actually an invitation into a revelation of His power.

The exploits we do as those who know the Lord must be ones of power, for that is the Gospel Jesus demonstrated. Our world needs Jesus, and He is power. If we are not giving people a Gospel of God's transforming power, then we are presenting something other the message of the cross,[46] and sadly they are getting more of us than Him. Greater levels of power come when we disregard our fear-of-man-based need to appear eloquent and give ourselves over to surrendered simplicity, resolving to know nothing but Christ and Him crucified.[47] That childlike simplicity of focus keeps us from muddying the message and deluding its power.[48] Operating in such open dependency on the Lord will cost us our dignity in the eyes of man, but knowing Him is our sufficiency.

---

[43] Matthew 6:10

[44] 2 Corinthians 5:20

[45] Matthew 10:7-8; Mark 16:15-18

[46] 1 Corinthians 1:18

[47] 1 Corinthians 2:2

[48] 1 Corinthians 1:17

***

Following in Jesus' footsteps is costly, but not complicated. When we know Him, we trust Him enough to risk entering into impossible situations, like Peter stepping out onto the water.[49] An awareness of His nearness emboldens us; our loving fear of Him restrains us from either quenching[50] or grieving[51] His Holy Spirit, which empowers our obedience. His power working through our weak humanity testifies to His glory and dumbfounds the wisdom of the world.

The willingness to intercede on behalf of our land, to yield as pliable vessels of His power, and to do the work of evangelists[52] will propel us as God's House of Prayer, the Church, into our prophetic destiny: an Isaiah-61 generation of people that arises in the time of the Lord's favor, anointed by His Spirit to proclaim the Good News and do evangelistic exploits of power.[53] God promises to help and hear us in this hour—it is imperative we do not waste the grace gifted to us for this significant assignment.[54] The harvest is ripe with people hungering after God,[55] His grace and favor are plentiful, and the time is now.

***

Holy Spirit proclaimed through the pen of Hosea that a day would come where "the earth will be filled

---

[49] Matthew 14:28

[50] 1 Thessalonians 5:19

[51] Ephesians 4:30

[52] 2 Timothy 4:5

[53] Isaiah 61:1-3

[54] 2 Corinthians 6:1-2; Isaiah 49:8

[55] Matthew 9:37; John 4:35

with the knowledge of the glory of the Lord, as the waters cover the sea."[56] What if our generation was the one that sees the prophecy come to pass? Knowing God's glorious nature—purely, experientially, and relationally, without the complacent veil of religion—is what both the establishment of the priesthood and the reaping of the harvest are unto. Imagine a time of great peace, where the Lord Himself teaches our children;[57] a time of reciprocated covenant, where no one needs to tell their neighbor "know God," because everyone knows Him.[58] Imagine everyone knowing Perfect Love.

Experiential knowledge of the Lord has a value that far surpasses anything else we could set our minds and hearts to in this life.[59] It is our portion, captivating us into a lifestyle of priestly worship and ministry to His heart. It is the inheritance we leave to our children. Our pursuit of the Lord should never spring from any motive besides intimacy; yet we need the wisdom to grasp that God knit us all together as His Body, each part reliant on the others. Our choices in regards to pursuing God in our individual lives have a greater impact on the Body and future generations than we can fathom.

**

Growing in the knowledge of God is effortless when we are in love with Him, and falling in love happens by simply leaning with meditative curiosity into what He has already revealed. Only in hungering after for Him do we find satisfaction—we feed on His daily-bread

---

[56] Hosea 2:14
[57] Isaiah 54:13
[58] Jeremiah 31:33-34
[59] Philippians 3:8

revelation with thankfulness, all the while allowing the not-yet-discovered facets of His beauty to allure us higher on His mountain of mystery.

Priests who never outgrow the basics of still fixation on His whisper and fear of the Lord live lives possessed by God. Each moment of their existence brims with the bliss of communion with Him and the thrilling adventure of exploring uncharted, holy territory. They know their God; He knows them. Oh, that we would be so overtaken by Him! Our ears should ever be tuned to His invitation and our hearts swift to remember His nearness when we drift from what He has revealed. Please do not forget: there is *more*, and He *wants* to be found. His majesty, goodness, and faithfulness transcend human imagination—the unknown depths of His nature beckon us to explore.

AFTERWORD

While I believe many of the truths of Scripture included in *The Divine Knowing* will always be relevant because His words will never pass away, a great deal of my inspiration in writing the book came from dreams, visions, and words the Lord has given me over the past year. Because of that, I believe there are things within this book that are specific and prophetic to the season we are currently in.

In worship one Sunday in September 2018, the Lord showed me a vision, and this is what I wrote that afternoon based on what I saw:

"It is my conviction that the fear of the Lord will hit entire cities. Individual believers and the Body at large will no longer compartmentalize themselves—secular and sacred lines will be broken when we realize that God abides everywhere, not just in church buildings. He is worthy of a holy habitation. Our cities will be bigger, brighter, and cleaner, both in the physical and the spiritual. God will use His lovers who fear Him throughout cities as 'conductors,' as both leaders and lightning rods, to send out His glory and power in the streets.

When the fear of the Lord fills us, we will look and act more like Jesus than ever before. Loving what He loves and hating what He hates—lifting people into an encounter with Him and allowing Him to crush Satan under our feet. The gravity of the healthy fear He's going to inspire in our hearts will make us aware of the seriousness of the times and keep us grounded, no matter what comes."

A few months later, Holy Spirit showed me through a dream and later reiterated it to me through a vision, that there were specific cities that would be revival hot spots in America—cities hit by the fear of the Lord unto mighty moves of God. In my dream on November 22, 2018, I was standing in a classroom of my childhood middle school, and on the classroom bulletin board was a map of the United States. The map was dark blue, and it showed locations where there were "fires." The fires were popped up all across the United States. I can't remember all of the locations, but I do remember California, Texas, Illinois, Florida, and New York having fires. I woke up feeling the map was showing where revival fires will pop up rather than natural fires.

Then on May 21, 2019, I was on a walk in one of my favorite places when the Lord began to speak to me distinctly. He said:

"Tent pegs are being expanded. The time is now. Certain cities hold the tent pegs. Redding, Los Angeles, New York City, Dallas, Orlando, and Nashville in the middle. You need to leave where you are to expand out. You bring expansion. Grasp the peg tightly as you expand out. Tension will come but don't stop pulling when you feel it. It is necessary. Keep going until I tell you to stop. There shall be no slack in My Kingdom. Mobilize the makeshift—mobilize and improvise. Improvise with excellence. Position yourself for provision for the vision. If the increase comes before you expand, where would the increase go? It would sit on the ground and waste. I am not wasteful. Make space for My proclamation to fill. It's impossible for Me to speak unfruitful words. My words are pregnant with provision. But I won't speak words that have weight that you can't carry. Expand. Expand. Expand."

In the months that followed, God began to unpack and zoom in on the picture He was painting of a mighty temple being erected over the United States. He showed me that individual believers who—in response to revelations of Who God is, His glory, His plans for His temple (Ezekiel 43-44)—answer the call to priesthood, to intimate prayer, and to worshipful ministry unto the Lord will be ones who help drive the "tent pegs" into the ground. And I found that driving tent pegs and taking new territory for the Lord in cities would begin with priests "driving tent pegs" within their own thinking. Priests will dismantle any thought that "sets itself up against the knowledge of God, taking every thought captive to make it obedient to Christ" (2 Corinthians 10:5), impaling those demonic, faithless thoughts with the truths of God's word.

The greatest battleground for believers is in the mind, but when that is recognized and the Church begins taking ground in the area of beliefs, there will be no stopping the explosion of the knowledge of the glory of God. When priests renew their mind in this way, being consecrated and transformed into Christ's image through intimate knowledge of Him, it will begin to infiltrate entire cites and the nation at large—such a priesthood who fear the Lord enough to pursue deeper knowledge of Him will be the "conductors" God spoke to me about in September 2018.

What the Lord is going to do in our nation is beyond anything we can imagine. I am filled with a deep conviction and an urgency that we must prepare now for what He wants to release—expanding out our inner capacities by answering the call to intimate priesthood, being transformed by the militant renewal of our mind and repentance from lies, and leaning into the tension of such expansion, trusting that He is found right in the middle of it all. We are being built into something beautiful. The discomfort and tension we embrace in our own lives is unto taking territory our children won't have to struggle to live in.

This is an Isaiah 54 season—a season of expansion. The expansion season won't last long, though, and then the great outpouring of His Spirit, the glorious revelation of His majesty, and a mighty soul harvest will come. 2020 will be a significant year of revival. He is going to fill our nation with the knowledge of His glory. The Bridegroom is setting us apart to be a nation of holy lovers of God, a nation that knows Him. We must prepare now.

"Sing, barren woman,
you who never bore a child;
burst into song, shout for joy,
you who were never in labor;
because more are the children of the desolate woman
than of her who has a husband,"
says the Lord.
[2] "Enlarge the place of your tent,
stretch your tent curtains wide,
do not hold back;
lengthen your cords,
strengthen your stakes.
[3] For you will spread out to the right and to the left;
your descendants will dispossess nations
and settle in their desolate cities.
[4] "Do not be afraid; you will not be put to shame.
Do not fear disgrace; you will not be humiliated.

You will forget the shame of your youth
   and remember no more the reproach of your
widowhood.
⁵ For your Maker is your husband—
   the Lord Almighty is his name—
the Holy One of Israel is your Redeemer;
   he is called the God of all the earth.
⁶ The Lord will call you back
   as if you were a wife deserted and distressed in spirit—
a wife who married young,
   only to be rejected," says your God.
⁷ "For a brief moment I abandoned you,
   but with deep compassion I will bring you back.
⁸ In a surge of anger
   I hid my face from you for a moment,
but with everlasting kindness
   I will have compassion on you,"
   says the Lord your Redeemer.
      ⁹ "To me this is like the days of Noah,
   when I swore that the waters of Noah would never
again cover the earth.
So now I have sworn not to be angry with you,
   never to rebuke you again.
¹⁰ Though the mountains be shaken
   and the hills be removed,
yet my unfailing love for you will not be shaken
   nor my covenant of peace be removed,"
   says the Lord, who has compassion on you.
      ¹¹ "Afflicted city, lashed by storms and not
comforted,
   I will rebuild you with stones of turquoise,
   your foundations with lapis lazuli.
¹² I will make your battlements of rubies,
   your gates of sparkling jewels,
   and all your walls of precious stones.

¹³ All your children will be taught by the Lord,
   and great will be their peace.
¹⁴ In righteousness you will be established:
Tyranny will be far from you;
   you will have nothing to fear.
Terror will be far removed;
   it will not come near you.
¹⁵ If anyone does attack you, it will not be my doing;
   whoever attacks you will surrender to you.
      ¹⁶ "See, it is I who created the blacksmith
   who fans the coals into flame
   and forges a weapon fit for its work.
And it is I who have created the destroyer to wreak
havoc;
¹⁷   no weapon forged against you will prevail,
   and you will refute every tongue that accuses you.
This is the heritage of the servants of the Lord,
   and this is their vindication from me,"
declares the Lord." (Isaiah 54, NIV)

May we be the generation that embraces this priestly mandate. May we be the generation that seeks the Lord, because He wants to be found and He is wonderful. There is nothing more worthwhile than pursuing Jesus and growing in the knowledge of Him. I pray Holy Spirit purifies our hearts that we might see the Lord more clearly and love Him as wholeheartedly as He deserves to be loved. Jesus is worthy!